EAST LOTHIAN at WAR

JACK TULLY-JACKSON and IAN BROWN

East Lothian
District Library

1996

Jack Tully-Jackson

In 1942 Dublin born Jack Tully-Jackson then a member of the A.T.C. and residing in Portrush, Northern Ireland volunteered for flying duties with the R.A.F. This frustrated teenage airman was directed to front line R.A.F. Electronic Listening Stations in South East England.

In January 1944 Jack was a member of a selected group of R.A.F. Regiment Airmen posted to R.A.F. Macmerry, East Lothian to be the R.A.F. element of "Fortitude North" deception controlled by M.I.6 from Edinburgh Castle in support of D. Day preparations designed to confuse the "Abwehr" into believing that an invasion of Norway was imminent. At the end of hostilities this R.A.F. Unit proceeded to the Norwegian Arctic to take charge of Luftwaffe Airfields.

On return to civilian life Jack settled in Haddington and for the past 25 years has become well known for his involvement in the production of Audio-Visual Programmes of local interest. This publication is the result of one of these projects.

Ian Brown

Ian Brown has been studying the history of the Second World War since the age of five, some 21 years ago. Ian has spent the last ten years researching the history of radar in Scotland and has amassed an extensive archive of thousands of photographs, documents and personal accounts. Through his work for the Historical Radar Archive, Ian has become the acknowledged authority on wartime ground radar in Scotland and northern England and has given a number of lectures to national and local organisations. Last summer Ian gained a Batchelor of Arts (Honours) degree in History from the University of Stirling and co-authored a guide to twentieth century defences in Britain. His third book, a history of wartime radar in Scotland, is due to be completed by the end of 1997. He is currently employed as a warehouseman but hopes to gain employment in a museum dealing with military or aviation history where his unique knowledge can be put to use.

My sincere thanks to Ian Brown, for his enthusiastic and professional support with this publication.
Jack Tully-Jackson

Designed and Printed by
East Lothian District Council

Published by
East Lothian District Library

ISBN 1 897857 15 2

© Jack Tully-Jackson and Ian Brown
1996

Foreword

East Lothian was a witness to the Second World War in Britain from the very beginning right until the end. Early photo reconnaissance missions were flown over the county and photos taken on 2 October 1939 still exist of the Forth Bridge and military installations around the Firth of Forth. The first air attack over Britain of the Second World War took place in the skies above Fife, Lothian and the Forth and another photo reconnaissance mission, on 28 October 1939, resulted in the first German aircraft to crash intact on British soil since the First World War, the bomber landing near Humbie.

Right from the start, East Lothian was in the front line and the county was to play an important part in the war effort throughout the war, as home to many units carrying out essential training, both airborne and ground, including troops from Poland. East Lothian also played an important part in the secret war, listening into the enemy radio messages, training members of the Special Operations Executive, and also being chosen as the location for deception operations which played a vital part in the success of the Normandy landings on D-Day, 6 June 1944.

The county continued to be in the front line right up until the end of the war in Europe. Late on the night of 7 May 1945, one hour before the German surrender officially began the Avondale Park and the Sneland 1 were sunk off the Isle of May by one of the newest types of German U-boat. Nine men were tragically killed on the two vessels, within sight both of land and of victory.

East Lothian also played a very important part in the fighting of the food front, which is hardly surprising for such a predominantly agricultural area. Virtually every piece of open land in the county was put under the plough in an attempt to make Britain as near self-sufficient as possible in the production of food. It was impossible to fight a war on an empty stomach and everyone from service personnel to factory girls to children benefited from the great increase in agricultural production in East Lothian.

This book cannot claim to be comprehensive, and only gives a few brief glimpses of what happened in East Lothian during the conflict of 1939-1945. It is hoped that in due course a more detailed book may be written which will give more information on the subjects covered here, and also on aspects which it was impossible to include, no matter how much we wished we could.

We would be very grateful for anyone with information about any aspect of East Lothian at War, whether it concerns the military units and bases in the county, the civilian services, prisoners of war or the Home Front, to contact us in the hope that we can include it in a future publication. At the very least, it would ensure that the information is recorded for the future and not lost as memories fade. If you have any information about Dirleton radar station or the radar trials at Tantallon, please contact Ian Brown at 3 Kingsmuir Crescent, Peebles EH45 9AB. For any other topics, please contact Jack Tully-Jackson at 14 Hawthornbank Road, Haddington EH41 3AU.

Contents

Acknowledgements

I would like to thank the following individuals and organisations for their assistance which proved of great importance in the production of this book.

Mr. James Abraham; Mrs. Greta Anderson; Mr. George Angus; Mr. Mike Bragg;
Mr. Joe Brown; Mrs M. Chalmers-Watson; Mrs Margaret Cheetham; Mrs Helen Cole;
Mr. Robert Cunninghame BEM; Mr. George Davidson;
Squadron Leader M. S. Dean, MBE; Mr. Harry Dittrich;
Misses Mary and Netta Dobson; Mr. Alaister Drysdale; Mr Stan Fedoryszyn;
Mr Ally Knox; Mr. B. C. Lyons; Mrs. Jean McEwan; Mr David McManus;
Mr. William Oldershaw; Mr R. John Steinberger; Mr. Ian Shaw; Mrs Helen Skakel;
Mr. Andrew Sommerville; Mr John Steele; Mrs. Mary Stenhouse; Miss Eunice Wilson.

I would also like to thank Jack Tully-Jackson for passing on his bulging files and for his invaluable assistance at all stages of the writing process, for it is his research which forms the basis for by far the greater part of this book.

Official Sources

Historical Radar Archive; Public Record Office;
Imperial War Museum; Defence Research Agency;
Scottish United Service Museum; R.A.F. Museum;,
Fleet Air Arm Museum; Scottish Museum of Flight;
The Archives of 602, 603, 607 and 614 R.A.F.V.R Squadrons Army H.Q. Scotland;
Mine Clearance Unit, Rosyth; Historic Scotland;
Scottish National Library; Edinburgh Central Library;
National Railway Museum; Scotsman Publications;
D.C. Thompson & Co.; Haddingtonshire Courier;
Eastleigh History Society; Southampton Hall of Aviation;
North Berwick Community Council; Dunbar Sea Cadets;
Gullane and Dirleton History Society;
British and Canadian War Graves Commission;
East Lothian Library and Museum Services.

One

Airfields

Macmerry Aerodrome

Edinburgh Flying Club began using Macmerry aerodrome, which was sometimes known as Tranent or Penston, in 1929. In this photo *(1a)* scouts from Tranent are seen during their visit to the field in 1938, which evidently included some instruction in the use of gas masks, a quite startling sign of the approaching world war. Nonetheless, this was still peacetime and from 1936 to 1939 North Eastern Airways operated some scheduled flights from Macmerry.

The landing ground was taken over by the Royal Air Force in 1941 and on 16 January a detachment of Hurricanes from No. 607 Squadron moved to Macmerry, rejoining the rest

1(a)

Tranent Scouts at Macmerry flying fields 1938

1(b)

*De Havilland 89A
of 614 (County of
Glamorgan)
Squadron,
Macmerry*

of the squadron at Drem on 2 March. Three days later, on 5 March 1941, No. 614 (County of Glamorgan) moved into Macmerry from Grangemouth, flying mainly Westland Lysanders and Bristol Blenheims, although there were also a number of miscellaneous types. One such was the de Havilland 89A Dominie *(see 1b)*, the military version of the de Havilland Dragon Rapide light airliner, which was used for a variety of communications duties. No 614 Squadron was an Army Co-operation squadron, carrying out such work as spotting for artillery units, reporting on any necessary corrections in the range and direction of the shelling, as well as general reconnaissance and even light bombing duties. At Macmerry, however, these duties were only training exercises, and it was only when detachments were sent south that squadron members were able to put their training to use.

At the end of May 1942 eight Blenheims from 614 Squadron were detached to West Raynham in Norfolk to carry out intruder attacks on Luftwaffe night fighter airfields in support of the 1000 bomber raid on Cologne on the night of 30/31

May 1942, the Blenheims returning to Macmerry soon after. Part of the squadron was again detached from Macmerry, in August 1942, to participate in the raid on Dieppe on 19 August.

In 1942 No. 614 Squadron was joined at Macmerry by several other Army Co-operation units. No. 13 Squadron was here for the first ten days of August 1942 with its Blenheims and No. 225 Squadron arrived on the last day of August for two months with Mustangs before heading for North Africa. On 21 November 1942 No. 63 Squadron found itself, with its Mustang aircraft, at Macmerry until moving to Turnhouse in July 1943, although a detachment remained at Macmerry for a few weeks. These units were involved in a number of local army exercises such as Exercise Dryshod which was held in early August 1942 in Ayrshire, a rehearsal for the landings at Dieppe which took place only a few days later. No. 13 Squadron was amongst the units which provided air support for the troops involved in the mock amphibious landing.

During 1942 Macmerry aerodrome was greatly expanded in size, extending onto the site

1(c)

Lysanders flying above clouds

of the First World War landing ground at Penston, used by No. 77 Squadron from 1916 until being disbanded in June 1919.

A great many other units used Macmerry at various times during the war. The Operational Training Units at East Fortune *(see 1d)* used Macmerry as a satellite station. From the beginning of 1943 the R.A.F. Regiment had a training school at Macmerry and from October 1943 to early 1944, 200 U.S. Army Air Force ground staff were based here, as was an Elementary Gliding School between April 1944 and 1946. Cunliffe-Owen Aircraft Limited had a factory on the aerodrome, the workforce of which were principally concerned with the repair of Lockheed Hudson aircraft *(see 14b and 14c)*.

Macmerry aerodrome also played an important part in the deception operations intended to make the German High Command believe that there was an invasion of Norway planned from Scotland *(see 13a and 13b)*.

On 21 April 1945 Macmerry was loaned by the R.A.F. to the Royal Navy, the intention being that No. 770 Squadron, Fleet Air Arm would use the aerodrome, although this did not, in fact, happen. However, Macmerry was commissioned on 1 June 1945 as a satellite of Drem *(see 1g)*, which was already being used by the Fleet Air Arm, Macmerry being allocated the name H.M.S. Nighthawk II. However, Macmerry was never actually used by the Fleet Air Arm and was returned to the R.A.F. on 15 March 1946.

Macmerry was reopened by the Edinburgh Flying Club on 31 August 1946, having gone full circle from its pre-war use, flying from here finally ending with the closure of the airfield in 1953.

East Fortune Aerodrome

1(d)

*Australian
Beaufighter Squadron
at East Fortune*

East Fortune is probably best known today as the home of the Museum of Flight and as the starting point of the first non-stop double crossing of the Atlantic, achieved by the airship R34 in July 1919. There had been an air station at East Fortune during the First World War, with both airships and aircraft operating from there after the opening of the station in September 1915.

Military flying was to be seen again at East Fortune during the Second World War, with the arrival in June 1941 of No. 60 Operational Training Unit (O.T.U.) from Yorkshire. This unit had been formed in April, the second O.T.U. set up to train night fighter crews for Fighter Command, work of vital importance in order to improve the strength of the defences against the night blitzes.

No 60 O.T.U. operated with ex-operational aircraft of the types used for night fighting, principally Bristol Blenheims and Beaufighters, and Boulton Paul Defiants, and the age of these aircraft was a major factor in the number of fatal crashes during training flights. The crews were often a long way from home, most of the trainees coming from Poland, New Zealand, Australia and Canada as well as Britain. In November 1942 it was decided that of the four night fighter O.T.U.s in existence by then, one should be disbanded, 60 O.T.U. being the unit chosen.

As a result, on 24 November 1942 East Fortune aerodrome was transferred to No. 17 Group, Coastal Command and training now began with No. 132 O.T.U. Training was now given for anti-shipping strikes using Beauforts and Beaufighters (see photo), these being the main anti-shipping strike aircraft then in use. From April 1944 training was also given using de Havilland Mosquito aircraft.

Crews trained at East Fortune played an important part in formations such as the Banff Strike Wing and the Dallachy Strike Wing, both based on the Moray coast to harass and attack German shipping along the Norwegian coast, work which was extremely dangerous as a result of attacks on heavily defended targets, but saw

Drem Aerodrome

Known at the time as West Fenton, there was a landing ground at Drem during the First World War, used by No. 77 Squadron for Home Defence in 1916 and 1917. Between April and August 1918 the American 41st Aero Squadron was based at West Fenton and on 15 April 1918

No. 2 Training Depot Station formed here, with Sopwith Pups, Camels and SE 5as until being disbanded in 1919, by which time West Fenton had been renamed Gullane.

Early in 1939 No. 13 Flying Training School (F.T.S.) formed at the aerodrome, by now

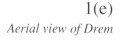

1(e)

Aerial view of Drem

renamed again as Drem, using Airspeed Oxfords, Hawker Harts and Audaxes, which could be seen day and night doing circuits of the aerodrome. The bulk of No. 13 F.T.S. left Drem early in October 1939, the unit being formally disbanded on 27 October, by which time war had broken out.

No. 602 (City of Glasgow) Squadron was an Auxiliary Air Force unit, which had been allocated Drem as its 'War Station', although the occupation of the aerodrome by No. 13 F.T.S. meant that it was not until 13 October that the squadron moved its Vickers-Supermarine Spitfire Mark Is to its new base. The auxiliaries arrived just in time, for it was only three days later that the first air battle took place in the skies above Britain in the shape of an attack on the afternoon of 16 October by twelve Junkers Ju 88 bombers against ships of the Royal Navy in the Firth of Forth. Spitfires of Nos. 602 and 603 Squadrons were scrambled from Drem and Turnhouse respectively, it being the Edinburgh Auxiliaries, No. 603 Squadron, who got the first kill, off Port Seton, followed ten minutes later by a Junkers 88 shot down off Crail by Flight Lieutenant Pinkerton of 602 Squadron. These two German aircraft were the first to be shot down over Britain since the First World War and resulted in a message being sent to Drem from the Commander-in-Chief of Fighter Command, Air Marshall Sir Hugh Dowding, "Well done. First blood to the Auxiliaries!"

Drem aerodrome was in an ideal position for the defence of Edinburgh and Rosyth from the continent and therefore saw a succession of day fighter squadrons. No 609 (West Riding) Squadron arrived the day after the auxiliaries had achieved their first kills, and was followed by 72 and 111 Squadrons later that year. German aircraft continued to meet their end in the vicinity of Drem, 602 Squadron having a hand in the shooting down of the Heinkel 111 at Humbie (see 4b, 4c, 4d, 4e and 4f) as well as several others in late 1939 and early 1940 from the Isle of May to St. Abb's Head.

Events were equally exciting on 28 February 1940 when His Royal Highness King George VI, accompanied by Air Marshall Dowding and the Air Officer Commanding No 13 Group (responsible for the fighter defence of Scotland and northern England) Air Vice-Marshal Saul, visited Drem. During his visit, the King presented the Commanding Officer of 602 Squadron, Wing Commander Douglas Farquhar, with the Distinguished Flying Cross.

The Battle of Britain in the summer of 1940 saw a succession of squadrons based at Drem, with some moving south to take part in the battle, whilst others came north for short rests. Whilst resting at Drem these squadrons would carry out convoy patrols, watching over the shipping steaming up the east coast, work which was uneventful and largely boring.

A number of night fighter units were based at Drem, beginning with No. 29 Squadron in April 1940. No. 600 (City of London) Squadron saw itself here in April 1941 and one of the squadron's Blenheims shot down a German bomber during

1(f)

602 (City of Glasgow) Squadron at Drem

1(g)
784 Squadron, F.A.A. at Drem

1(h)
Parachute Cafe, Drem

the bombing of Clydeside that month. No. 605 (County of Warwick) Squadron used Drem as a forward aerodrome for Mosquito intruder flights, the unit's home base being Castle Camps on the Essex/Cambridgeshire border. One success was achieved from Drem on the night of 16 June 1943, when an enemy aircraft, believed to be a Heinkel He 177 four-engined bomber, was shot down over Denmark.

The aerodrome gradually saw a great number of night fighter units based here, the longest resident being not an R.A.F. but Fleet Air Arm unit, No. 784 Squadron *(see 1g)*. The squadron moved to Drem on 18 October 1942 where it carried out its work as a night fighter school, training naval aircrews in the techniques necessary to fly and fight by night. Ground control for this training, which would guide the fighter under training into its target, was provided by Dirleton Ground Control of Interception radar station *(see 6b)*, with another station at Cockburnspath handling interceptions at low-level out to sea.

Drem was, in fact, to be taken over completely by the Royal Navy on 21 April 1945 and was commissioned as H.M.S. Nighthawk two months later, in conformity with the naval policy of allocating names to all naval shore establishments.

In the meantime, however, another night fighter unit, No. 1692 (Radio Development) Flight formed at Drem on 5 July 1943. This was a most interesting unit and was part of No. 100 Group, which was responsible for countermeasures to German radar and radio equipment. The work of No. 1692 Flight involved trials of a considerable number of airborne radar sets and various jamming equipment, as well as the techniques best suited to their use. The flight was equipped with a wide variety of aircraft including the main types used as night fighters.

Drem was also a pioneer in another field: aerodrome lighting. When No. 602 (City of Glasgow) Squadron carried out patrols from Drem during 1940, it was found that the flare from the exhaust made the pilot's view on final approach to the runway very poor indeed at night. However, it was discovered that if dim lamps were placed in alignment with the curving approach of a normal landing in a Spitfire, it was much simpler for the pilot to stick to the correct approach path and make a successful landing.

This system was such a success that the so-called 'Drem lighting' system became the basis of all R.A.F. aerodrome lighting.

The Q-site, a dummy landing ground with electrical lighting set up to represent the runway flarepaths, intended to deceive enemy night bombers into believing they had found Drem, had been set up at Whitekirk and Halls farm, and had attracted quite a number of bombs. The decoy was not intended to work during the daytime and thus Drem found itself the target of unwanted attention on 12 August 1942 when a Junkers Ju 88 bombed the aerodrome. Luckily, there were no injuries but the control tower and several Spitfires were damaged.

Drem was to be witness to one of the most dramatic scenes at the end of the war in Europe when, on 11 May 1945, Spitfires of No. 603 (City of Edinburgh) Squadron intercepted three Junkers Ju 52 transport aircraft which were flying from Stavanger to Drem, the fighters escorting the German aircraft into the aerodrome. These three aircraft, painted white, carried a German delegation to arrange the surrender of German forces in Norway. The German officers were driven in a great variety of staff cars, with a very large motorcycle escort, from Drem to Edinburgh Castle. The Junkers 52s were later flown away from Drem and it is very likely that they were used in the early post-war period as commercial airliners.

On 15 March 1946 Drem was returned to R.A.F. control, although it is not thought that the R.A.F. used the aerodrome after taking it over again.

Two

Satellite Landing Ground

Lennoxlove S.L.G.

During January 1941 the R.A.F. authorised work to be carried out to prepare part of the estates of Colstoun and Lennoxlove for use as No. 27 Satellite Landing Ground (S.L.G.)

The role of R.A.F. Lennoxlove S.L.G. was as a secret place for the storage of replacement aircraft, where the enemy would be unaware of their presence and the aircraft would therefore be safe from attack. The landing ground was to be part of No. 18 Maintenance Unit (M.U.) which was based at R.A.F. Dumfries.

Work extended from January to April, with permission being gained from the Chief Constable at Haddington to close by means of

2(a)

Huts at Lennoxlove

self-shutting gates at each end, a small road running across the landing strip. Finally, on 24 April 1941 a Fairey Battle light bomber made a trial landing at Lennoxlove which proved successful and the landing ground was declared acceptable.

On 25 April a Bristol Blenheim was flown in, the first aircraft delivered to be stored at No. 27 S.L.G. However, despite this achievement it was decided that only smaller aircraft, such as Hurricanes, could be stored at Lennoxlove because the landing strip had not been extended, this being due to delays in getting permission to close the road separating the extension from the rest of the landing ground. However, some progress was made, and by the end of May 1941 all flight equipment huts were complete and a telephone line had been installed at the headquarters office. Additionally, an Army guard of one officer, two N.C.O.s and 12 men of the 10th Royal Scots was billeted in Lennoxlove House.

Permission to close the road necessary to extend the landing strip was not slow in being given by Haddington Police and once the work was completed, which included lowering the surface level of the road to avoid it sitting proud of the grass runway, many more Blenheims were flown in to Lennoxlove.

The Commanding Officer of No. 18 M.U. visited Lennoxlove in August 1941 and gave some thought to the possibility of landing Westland Whirlwind twin-engined fighters there. The unit's Chief Test Pilot mentioned that the Whirlwind swung badly in crosswinds but was nonetheless prepared to attempt a landing when the wind conditions were considered suitable. This was carried out very successfully and, as a result, many Whirlwinds came to be stored at Lennoxlove. Even larger aircraft were to be flown in to the S.L.G., with Vickers Wellington bombers *(see 2b)* making their first appearance in

2(b)

Lennoxlove S.L.G. with a/c

late 1941, and even a Handly-Page Halifax four-engined heavy bomber landing here in the summer of 1942, the S.L.G. being declared ideal for such large aircraft.

By November 1944 No. 27 S.L.G. had 119 aircraft in storage, most of which were Wellingtons. Quite a number of these suffered damage as a result of branches falling from the trees under which they were hidden, and even from trees themselves, uprooted during gales.

In the summer of 1945 Lennoxlove gained a unique distinction. A derivative of the Whirlwind fighter was the Westland Welkin which was designed as a high-altitude day and night fighter, intended for intercepting German bombers flying at great heights. This threat did not materialise and thus the Welkin never saw operational service. However, 67 Welkins were produced (as well as two prototypes), most of these being flown in to Lennoxlove for storage at the end of the war, before being scrapped.

The end of No. 27 S.L.G. followed not long afterwards, beginning in August 1945 and ending with the closure of the unit the following month.

Three

Flying Accidents

Ferny Ness Flying Accident

In the afternoon of Tuesday 27 April 1943 practice dive bombing was being carried out by Fleet Air Arm aircraft in co-operation with the Naval gunnery practice range at Ferny Ness Point between Longniddry and Aberlady. Around 4.00 pm, a dive bomber carried out two dives over the range, on the second of which the pilot seemed unable to pull out of the dive, crashing into the ground a few yards in front of a stationary S.M.T. bus. The aircraft then bounced and hit the bus, which had been hired to transport naval personnel to and from the range, and was just about to depart. Burning fuel from the aircraft set fire to the bus and it was quickly enveloped in flames.

In one of the most tragic accidents ever seen in East Lothian, 14 lives were lost. The pilot, Sub-Lieutenant Kenneth Jolly and Drogue Operator, Acting Leading Airman Robert Hartley, were both killed outright, as was the driver of the bus, David Mathieson. Ten naval ratings were killed, or died of their injuries, as well as Lewis Hiram Carpenter, a seaman in the U.S. Merchant Navy.

The National Fire Service pump from Haddington arrived at the scene of the accident as did ambulances from the nearby Polish Red Cross hospital. Some of the injured were taken to the Polish hospital and some in British Army vehicles to Gosford Camp. Many were severely burned and required extensive, and long-term, treatment for their injuries at the Astley-Ainslie Hospital.

The accident at Ferny Ness was a great tragedy, presenting a scene which one witness compared to his experiences of the Battle of Arras in 1917.

3(a)

Ferny Ness Headline

EVENING DISPATCH, Wednesday, April 28, 1943

PLANE CRASHED INTO BUS

11 Dead in South-East Scotland Accident

Eleven lives were lost through an aeroplane crashing into a motor bus in South-East Scotland yesterday afternoon. The accident took place close

The loud rending noise of the crash was heard half a mile away. Helpers were soon on the spot, and intimation of the accident was made to the police.

Rushed to Hospital

Beechhill House Flying Accident

the Germans suffer heavily.

At about 11.00 p.m. on the night of Sunday, 22 October 1944 a Mosquito of No. 132 Operational Training Unit based at East Fortune was on a training flight when one of its fuel tanks exploded, the aircraft disintegrating and crashing into Beechhill House, two miles south-east of Haddington. Six people died in the accident, of which two were the crew of the aircraft. Mrs. Ruth de Pree, her brother Lieutenant-Colonel John Haig, D.S.O., her grandson David Pitcairn and the nurse, Daisy Spiers, were killed when the aircraft hit the house, although seven other family members and staff who were in the house at the time were lucky enough to escape injury. Mrs. de Pree was the eldest daughter of Mr. Hugh Veitch Haig, brother of Field-Marshal Earl Haig. She had been forced to leave her home at Saughton House in Edinburgh as a result of a fire which broke out there, and it was at that time that Mrs. de Pree had secured Beechhill House.

The Mosquito apparently struck a tree and was diverted in its course, demolishing 20 feet of a wall dividing the flower garden from the kitchen garden. One of the engines, along with part of a wing, were found in the kitchen garden. The other engine was found in the middle of a field 250 yards away from the house, and part of the undercarriage landed nearly quarter of a mile away.

When the aircraft wreckage hit Beechhill House, it immediately set the house on fire, part of the west wall having collapsed and the west wing being totally wrecked *(see 3b and 3c)*. The fire also prevented all attempts at rescue, despite Lieutenant-Colonel de Pree and the gardener, Mr. Francis Mortimer, trying to enter the house using a ladder. Lieutenant-Colonel Haig had been in a downstairs room at the time of the crash, ran to

his sister's room, and was not seen again.

Firemen from Haddington and a nearby aerodrome, probably Macmerry, arrived on the scene and, with the Edinburgh Brigade which arrived 25 minutes later, were able to save the servants' quarters and several rooms in the main house. They also prevented Mrs. Goda Pitcairn, daughter of Lieutenant-Colonel de Pree and mother of David Pitcairn, from dashing into the house, almost certainly saving her life by doing so. The cook, Mrs. Sarah Baxter, was thrown out of bed by the force of the crash and just had time to gather her $3^1/2$ year-old son Jackie and escape as flames began shooting along the passage towards the part of the house in which they were sleeping.

The ruined wing of the house continued to smoulder into the late afternoon of the following day whilst National Fire Service (N.F.S.) men turned over the rubble. The Haddington A.R.P. Rescue and Repair Service and the Leith N.F.S. Salvage Corps were employed on the burned-out

3(b)

Beechhill House - morning after

N.F.S. men searching the debris in the burnt-out wing of the house.

fabric of the house. Dr. Campbell, Medical Officer for the County of East Lothian, spent Monday afternoon identifying the bodies, only three of which had been recovered. The body of Lieutenant-Colonel Haig had not been found.

The tragic accident at Beechhill House was the worst involving an aircraft flying from East Fortune during the Second World War and was particularly deeply felt because of the loss of such prestigious community figures.

3(c)
Beechhill

Mr William Moffat, G.M.

Mr. William Moffat, a farmer from Buxley Farm, Tranent, was awarded the George Medal for his bravery in rescuing the pilot of a Hawker Hurricane which made a forced landing. The aircraft struck a low wall and hedge, the wing then catching the tie lines of a metal radio mast, and by the time that Mr. Moffat reached the scene, accompanied by Mr. Hugh Kenny, Mr. Alexander Little, Mr. John Geddes and Mr. John Pearson, the aircraft had caught fire and was well alight. The pilot was apparently held fast by his seat harness and his flying suit and hair were on fire. Mr. Moffat, with the assistance of the other men, managed to cut the straps and lift the pilot out of the cockpit. The pilot was still conscious and, having warned the men of the possibility of explosion, they wrapped him in a jacket and carried him a short distance from the aircraft and were only just clear of the wreckage when the fuel tank exploded, setting off the aircraft's machine-gun ammunition. The pilot was carried to the shelter of a shed at Buxley Farm and Mr.

3(d) *Mr William Moffat G.M.*

Moffat then telephoned for an ambulance and a doctor. The pilot was taken to hospital, although he tragically died the following day of his injuries.

Four

Crashed German Aircraft

Humbie Heinkel 111

From almost the very outbreak of war, German reconnaissance aircraft were flying over the Firth of Forth, photographing principally shipping movements but also military installations and defences. These aircraft had a bank of cameras fitted to the bomb racks under their port wing, the other wing carrying its load of bombs, should the opportunity arise to attack British ships. On 16 October 1939 an air raid was launched against ships in the Firth of Forth, resulting in two German bombers being shot down, one crashing in the sea near Crail and the other off Port Seton. On 22 October a Heinkel 111 bomber was shot down into the sea near St. Abb's Head during a reconnaissance mission.

Another reconnaissance mission took place on the morning of 28 October 1939, the Heinkel 111 coded 1H+JA of Kampfgeschwader 26 heading for the Firth of Clyde to photograph shipping, returning via the Firth of Forth to carry out the same duties there. However, the aircraft had been detected by early warning radar and Spitfires of Nos. 602 (City of Glasgow) and 603 (City of Edinburgh) Squadrons, based at Drem and Turnhouse respectively, were scrambled to intercept.

The bomber was spotted over the Inchkeith, surrounded by bursts of anti-aircraft fire from ships of the Royal Navy in the estuary, and was chased by the fighters over Prestonpans and Tranent, successive attacks riddling the aircraft with around 300 bullets. Two of the four-man crew were killed, namely Corporal Bruno Reimann and Sergeant Gottleib Kowalke. The Heinkel was badly damaged, with shattered instruments and damaged controls. Then the port engine was hit, followed by the starboard. Without power, escape was impossible and the only option available was to glide the aircraft into a crash landing, as the navigator, Flying Officer Rolf Neihoff, ordered the pilot, Sergeant Kurt Lehmkuhl, to do. The pilot showed considerable skill in that he was able to almost stall the aircraft, reducing its speed as much as possible before touching down. Nonetheless, the tail of the aircraft hit a dry stane dyke, which tore off the starboard tailplane, and skidded several yards before coming to rest on Kidlaw Hill, between High Latch and Kidlaw Farm, 3 miles east of Humbie.

The navigator helped the injured pilot out of the aircraft, who was carried down the hill on a gate by farmworkers from Long Newton Farm. It was later discovered that the apparently uninjured Flying Officer Neihoff *(seen in 4c holding his back, with Police Sergeant Tait)* actually had a broken back as a result of the impact of the crash. The two dead crewmen were taken to Edinburgh and were buried in Portobello Cemetery on 31 October 1939, being reburied in the 1960s in the German servicemen's cemetery at Cannock Chase in Staffordshire.

4(a)
Ring belonging to German pilot

4(b)
*Heinkel 111 at Kidlaw,
Humbie*

4(c) *Pilot and Sgt. Tait* →

← 4(d) *Nose of Heinkel 111*

The crashed bomber proved of considerable local interest, with many locals making sightseeing trips. Not surprisingly though, in view of the fact that the Heinkel was the first enemy aircraft to land intact in Britain during the Second World War, Royal Air Force Intelligence were particularly interested in the wreck. On 31 October, the same day as the burial of the two crewmen, No. 63 Maintenance Unit based at Carluke began to dismantle the aircraft, the sections being transported to the Royal Aircraft Establishment at Farnborough. Once there a detailed examination took place which lasted until August 1941 and resulted in a 59 page report. The Heinkel's engines were removed from the crash site and taken by a local haulage contractor to Rolls-Royce at Hillingdon in Glasgow and from there to the Rolls-Royce works in Derby for evaluation. Willie Gilmarpin *(second from left in bowler hat, see 4e)* was the Rolls-Royce engineer sent to collect one of the engines. The work at Derby began in mid-November 1939, ending on 13 January 1940 when the Jumo 211A engine blew up during the testing.

The Humbie Heinkel was, however, to play a much more important role later that year By early 1940 Professor R. V. Jones of Air Intelligence, part of M.I.6, was convinced that the Germans had developed a navigational beam which they could use to accurately bomb targets, even when they were obscured by cloud. Having received a fcw clues about a system named Knickebein, he asked a colleague his theories. He recalls in his book, Most Secret War:

He duly interrogated the prisoners without at first getting anything of value. But when the prisoners were alone, one of them said to another that no matter how hard we looked we would never find the equipment. This could not have been a better challenge because it implied that the equipment was, in fact, under our noses, but that we would not recognise it. I therefore obtained a

4(e)

Aircraft being taken to Rolls-Royce factory, Glasgow. Headline from newscutting

copy of the full technical examination of the Heinkel 111 that had been shot down in the Firth of Forth raid, and looked especially at the various items of radio equipment. The only item that could possibly fill the bill was the receiver that was carried on the aircraft for the normal purpose of blind landing on the Lorenz beam system, which was now standard at many aerodromes. I ascertained that the radio equipment had been evaluated by N. Cox Walker at Farnborough and so I telephoned him. "Tell me, is there anything unusual about the blind landing receiver?" I asked. "No," he replied - and then, "but now you mention it, it is much more sensitive than they would ever need for blind landing." So that was it. I now knew the receiver, and the frequencies to which it could be tuned, and therefore on which the Knickebein beam must operate.

The Heinkel 111 which crashed near Humbie on 28 October 1939 is of great significance, not simply because it was the first enemy aircraft to land intact on British soil during the war, but because it provided the clues which were crucial to the detection and eventual jamming of the Knickebein blind bombing system which might otherwise have devastated Britain's cities and war industries. The devastation in Coventry on the night of 14/15 November 1940 was the result of the use of this system when, for various reasons, it was not possible to jam the beam. This is a perfect example of what might have been repeated the length and breadth of Britain had it not been for that interception in the skies over East Lothian.

North Berwick Heinkel 111

On 9 February 1940 another Heinkel 111 of Kampfgeschwader 26, which was based at Westerland aerodrome on the island of Sylt off the coast of northern Germany, crash landed in East Lothian. By then Luftwaffe crews had apparently nicknamed the Firth of Forth 'Suicide Corner', due to the number of German aircraft which had been shot down in that area. This particular aircraft, coded 1H+EN, was shot down by a Spitfire of No. 602 Squadron, piloted by Squadron Leader Douglas Farquhar. Firing 625 rounds at the Heinkel over Fife, smoke began to pour out of its port engine as it headed for the coast.

Critically damaged, it was clear that the aircraft would be unable to return across the North Sea to base, and so the pilot, Sergeant Helmut Meyer, made a forced landing at Rhodes Farm near North Berwick. This was almost perfect, the only blemish being that the aircraft hit a low hedge at the end of the landing and tipped over onto its nose. Only the rear gunner, Sergeant Wieners, was killed by the gunfire from Farquhar's Spitfire, and the rest of the crew climbed out of the aircraft without major injury. No. 165 Officer Cadet Training Unit was based in North Berwick, and the Commanding Officer, Lieutenant-Colonel H. E. Smith, sent an armed guard of 1 officer and 12 men to the crash site, in case of any trouble. However, the men arrived to find the aircrew had been taken prisoner by the local police. On the extreme right (see 4f) can be seen the bell tent which accommodated the R.A.F. personnel who were sent to guard the aircraft.

The minor damage to the Heinkel was repaired and the aircraft, with the outer wing section and engines removed, was taken by road through North Berwick and on to Drem. From there it was flown, with R.A.F. fighter escort, to the Royal Aircraft Establishment at Farnborough for evaluation. As the Heinkel was fully airworthy, it was allocated an R.A.F. serial number, AW177. Trials were carried out on the aircraft by both the R.A.F. and the Aeroplane and Armament Experimental Establishment at Boscombe Down.

In September 1941 Heinkel 111 AW177 was transferred to the Air Fighting Development Unit based at Duxford in Cambridgeshire. This unit

4(f)

*Heinkel 111
at North Berwick*

4(g)

Heinkel 111 being transported along Dirleton Avenue

4(h)

Heinkel 111 with R.A.F. personnel

had been formed to compare the relative performance of Allied and enemy aircraft and the Heinkel was operated by them until the formation in November 1941 of No. 1426 (Enemy Aircraft) Flight, when the Heinkel became the unit's first aircraft. No. 1426 Flight was formed in the belief that if certain pilots were able to fly German aircraft regularly, they would quickly become knowledgeable of the performance of the aircraft. Thus, accidents would be minimised and the pilots would become experienced enough to compare the relative performance of different types. The unit also toured round operational aerodromes in order to give regular aircrews greater exprcience of the appearance and tactics of enemy aircraft. The first such tour began on 11 February 1942, almost exactly two years since the Heinkel 111 had made its emergency landing near North Berwick. The aircraft also became a film star, appearing alongside Captain Clark Gable in Combat America, a training film for gunners in American aircraft.

The tours of U.S. airfields meant a busy schedule for No. 1426 Flight, but despite this the unit had been fortunate enough to avoid serious accident. That luck changed on Tour No. 10 when, on 10 November 1943, the Heinkel 111, accompanied by a Junkers 88 bomber and a Messerschmitt 109 fighter arrived at Polebrook airfield in Northamptonshire for the benefit of the 351st Bomb Group. Approaching the airfield, the Heinkel 111 and the Junkers 88 came in to land at opposite ends of the same runway. In order to avoid a head-on collision, the pilot of the Heinkel opened his throttles and climbed steeply to port. However, the climb was too steep and the aircraft stalled, going into a vertical spin, exploding on impact. Seven of the eleven men on board were killed in the tragedy.

Five

The Bombing of East Lothian

Ravensheugh Sands U.X.B.

On 2 May 1941 an unexploded bomb was discovered on the beach at about the high water mark at the south-east end of Ravensheugh Sands. No damage was caused and no-one was injured. This was a minor incident although U.X.B.s could pose a serious problem, in that they had to be safely disposed of and there was the potential that they could explode at any time, since some were fitted with a time delay mechanism. As a result, by making areas dangerous to enter until the bomb had been dealt with, U.X.B.s often caused greater problems than bombs which did detonate on impact.

East Lothian was to see a considerable number of bombs dropped within the county boundaries during the war years. In fact, between 1939 and 1945 a total of 185 high explosive bombs and 3 parachute mines, with 16 unexploded bombs, were dropped, as a result of which 3 people were killed and 22 injured, and one sheep was killed. Whilst these statistics are small in comparison with London, Coventry and Clydeside, they are tragic nonetheless, and are quite high for a rural area away from large cities.

5(a)
Ravensheugh U.X.B.

Traprain Law

5(b)
Traprain

On 24 July 1940 two German parachute mines landed at the east end of Traprain Law, 200 yards east of Traprain Law Quarry. One of the two mines exploded at the side of the road and burst a water main and brought down telephone lines, producing a crater which measured 25 feet across and was 15 feet deep. Mr. Rutherford, the road foreman, can be seen in the photograph. The other mine landed in a nearby potato field.

These mines were jettisoned as a result of a combat at 12.35 a.m. on the morning of the 24th when Sergeant Andy MacDowall of No. 602 Squadron, on night patrol, saw a Heinkel 111 caught in searchlight beams at East Linton. Making a head-on attack on the enemy bomber, Sergeant MacDowall saw tracer entering the Heinkel, which immediately jettisoned its two mines.

Observing the two parachutes descending, a rather agitated signalman at East Linton telephoned Waverley station to report that two parachutists had landed nearby and were throwing stones at his window! Even the crew of an ack-ack battery at Whitekirk believed that enemy parachutists had landed in East Lothian. It did not take long, however, to resolve the confusion and discover what had really been on the end of those parachutes!

The Bombing of Haddington 3 March 1941

5(c)
*Haddington
Pringles*

5(d)
*Haddington
Baillies*

At around 8.30 p.m on 3 March 1941 the air raid sirens sounded in Haddington and about half an hour later a stick of six high explosive bombs were dropped in the town, the most serious damage being done to the gift shop of Mr. Richard Baillie *(see 5d)* on the south side of Market Street which was completely burnt out. On the south side of Mr. Baillie's shop were the Women's Rural Institute rooms which were also hit, the bomb landing just after the conclusion of a meeting of the Women's Guild. Some of the women were caught in the blast just as they reached the street and one of them was injured. One bomb scored a direct hit on a building at the corner of Victoria Terrace and Hardgate, within 20 yards of The New County Cinema, which was full at the time. Another fell within the rear premises of an ironmonger's shop in Market Street which were demolished, and one bomb struck Halliday's Garage in Market Street, which was occupied as a store by the military, and set it on fire. Another bomb exploded in the middle of the road outside Cumming's draper's shop, Market Street, producing a crater 12 feet wide and 4 feet deep, as a result of which gas and water mains were burst. Market Street was blocked by debris for a considerable time.

One of the bombs did not explode, this being the one which struck the corner of the offices of the Haddingtonshire Courier, penetrating a brick wall and finishing up on the main door of a house above Pringle's butcher's shop in Market Street.

Incendiary bombs were dropped in Amisfield Park which was occupied by the military at that time (see 20a). The bombing of Haddington had started fierce fires and it became obvious that the Haddington National Fire Service would require assistance. The first two requests for help were ignored as they were not made through proper channels, despite the fact that a building used to store ammunition and Molotov cocktails was under threat!

The girls operating the telephone exchange showed great bravery in continuing to man the equipment throughout the attack, despite the fact that it was next door to Baillie's shop which was ablaze and by the time firemen reached the room, the girls were still passing calls while the curtains behind them were fiercely ablaze.

The all clear was sounded around 9.30 p.m., but in the space of half an hour, two people, one of them a soldier, had lost their lives and nineteen others were injured, mostly as a result of being hit by flying debris. The two who died that night were John Moggie of Amisfield Stables and Sergeant J. Mathieson of the 52nd Division. Tragically, Private James Taylor died later as a result of wounds he received from the bomb which landed on Mr. Baillie's shop.

On the afternoon of 4 March Haddington was visited by Lord Rosebery, Regional Commissioner for Civil Defence in Scotland, and Major Barclay Brown, Senior Regional Officer for Scotland, who made a tour of inspection of the bombed area. Lord Rosebery and Major Brown, accompanied by Air Raid Precautions officials, inspected the damage and talked to people who had been evacuated from their homes.

Six

Aircraft Tracking

Garvald Observer Corps Post

In the last few years prior to the outbreak of war in September 1939 the Royal Air Force implemented hurried preparations for the defence of Britain from air attack. As part of these steps, the Observer Corps (renamed Royal Observer Corps in 1941) organisation saw considerable expansion. One of the posts to open during this period was Baker 3 in No. 31 Observer Group, at Garvald, which came into use in February 1937 *(see 6a)*. Other posts in East Lothian were at Aberlady, Athelstaneford, Dunbar, Humbie, North Berwick and Tranent.

With the extensive enemy aerial activity in the Firth of Forth area during the early months of the war, the posts in East Lothian were kept busy. The posts in the area plotted well during the raid on the Forth on 16 October 1939 and on 28 October the Heinkel 111 which crashed near Humbie *(see 4b)* was tracked by the Humbie post itself.

The East Lothian R.O.C. were busy tracking aircraft throughout the war and, on 5 May 1944, the Garvald post tracked a very low-flying hostile bomber, probably a Junkers 88, which machine-gunned as it flew over on a south-easterly course.

Although the Royal Observer Corps (R.O.C.) has been criticised, not least by Churchill who considered it as representing stone age technology when compared to radar, at that time radar could not track low-flying aircraft overland because of the reflections picked up from the ground. The R.O.C. was vital to the raid reporting network in that it could follow aircraft inland even at night, and was able to give better indications of the numbers in large formations than radar could. The R.O.C. was, until its stand down on 12 May 1945, an essential element of the air defence organisation and the East Lothian posts played their part in the organisation.

6(a)
Garvald Observer Corps

Dirleton G.C.I.

6(b)

Dirleton G.C.I. personnel

In April 1941 a mobile Ground Control of Interception (G.C.I.) station was set up at Dirleton. This station was, as its name suggests, to provide ground control for night fighters trying to intercept German bombers in the area, directing the fighter towards its target until the German aircraft could be picked up by the radar onboard the fighter, which would then close in for the kill.

The equipment was initially housed in lorries with the aerials on wheeled caravans but this was replaced in the summer of 1942 by wooden hutting. A more permanent station became operational in October 1943 housed in a large brick Operations Block, which greatly improved the performance of the station. The capabilities of the station were further enhanced by June 1945 when installation was completed of additional radars which were much more accurate.

However, by the time that Dirleton was completed, the night blitz was over and there were few German bombers in the night sky over East Lothian. Much of the work at Dirleton was therefore devoted to training, working with the night fighter units in the area such as No. 60 Operational Training Unit, which trained R.A.F. night fighter crews and was based at East Fortune *(see 1d)*, and No. 784 Squadron, Fleet Air Arm at Drem *(see section 1g)*, which carried out much the same function for the Fleet Air Arm.

With the end of the war there was no hostile threat, and little need for training work either, so a gradual reduction in the staff of the station took place, the W.A.A.F. Radar Operators being posted away in December 1945. Dirleton G.C.I. itself closed down in March 1946 although it was used by No 3603 (City of Edinburgh) Fighter Control Unit for training at weekends during the late 1940s until 1954, when a new station opened at Anstruther.

No 405 Searchlight Company

In 1938 the 4th/5th Battalion, The Queen's Edinburgh Royal Scots was remustered as a Searchlight Regiment, the three companies of the battalion being renamed 405, 406 and 407 Searchlight Companies.

405 Company, commended by Major J. B. Allan, spent July 1939 in camp at Crossgates in Fife, much training being carried out at that time. When mobilisation was ordered on 1 September 1939 the companies deployed to their war stations, 405 Company moving to sites in East Lothian and part of Berwickshire, with its headquarters at Clerkington House, just south of Haddington *(see 6c, 6d and 6e)*.

The men in the Searchlight Companies were not a little unhappy in their role. The Royal Scots having an unbroken history as rifles and infantry since 1859, they were none too keen to find themselves armed with searchlights instead of rifles when war broke out. However, the air raid on shipping in the Firth of Forth on 16 October 1939 found them the first home unit to fire on the enemy, as a result of shots fired from a Lewis gun at a searchlight position in Midlothian.

Twelve days later, on 28 October, the first German aircraft to be brought down intact crash landed near Humbie, close to one of the sites operated by a detachment from 405 Company. The two surviving members of the bomber crew were taken prisoner by the territorials. It was recalled that the pilot had no doubt in his mind whatsoever that Germany would have won the

6(c)

No. 405 Searchlight Unit Clerkington House H.Q.

war by Christmas and that by then he would be back home a free man. Little was he to know that he faced six or seven years in captivity.

On 1 August 1940 the territorials became the 52nd Searchlight Regiment, Royal Artillery, but retained the sub-title Queen's Edinburgh Royal Scots. With this reorganisation, 405 Company was renamed 405 Battery.

Long and hard training continued throughout 1940 and 1941, at the same time as the units being continuously on duty. Life was far from easy on the cold and often remote sites during the winter, and it was a particularly arduous task starting a half-frozen generator on a cold night in order to power the searchlight.

The searchlights saw occasional action during 1940, illuminating enemy aircraft in the vicinity of the Firth of Forth at night and in poor weather. The sites were also busy on the night of 13/14 March 1941 when many German bombers heading for Clydeside were illuminated, though on most occasions there were no ack-ack guns or fighters to attack the bombers spotted by the searchlights. Nonetheless, the Station Commander at Drem sent a message of thanks the morning after two enemy aircraft were shot down as a result of their having been caught in searchlight beams. Both actions had taken place above dense cloud through which the searchlights had penetrated, and the searchlight companies were gratified to receive thanks for their efforts.

In early 1941 the tactical layout was changed from having single searchlights at each site, to three light clusters. In addition, there was one special six-light site in a field on the north side of Dirleton, which was known as 'Elsie'. On several occasions this site was bombed and machine-gunned, but no casualties were sustained as a result. Tragically though, one gunner was killed when he strayed into a minefield on Archerfield Golf Course.

Orders were received in August 1941 for 405 Battery to proceed overseas, a development of

intense pride to the regiment, since no Searchlight Battery in the 3rd A.A. Corps had received such orders before. At the last moment, the numbers required were reduced to 200, the balance to be made up from native troops upon arrival overseas. The selection of the 200 men was no simple task, but the choice was eventually made and they left Haddington on 11 October 1941 for the mobilisation centre in Southend.

6(d) and 6(e)

Clerkington Gardens (top)
and
Searchlight at Clerkington Gardens (above)

Seven

Anti-Invasion Defences

7(a)

Anti-tank cubes and cylinders at Belhaven

During 1940 and 1941, when Britain faced the very real threat of invasion from the continent, plans were implemented for the construction of extensive fixed defences along vulnerable stretches of coastline, important road junctions and river crossings. Much of this work was carried out in south-east England which was only a few miles away from the French coast and was considered the most likely location for a German invasion attempt.

However, the beaches of East Lothian were considered particularly suitable for amphibious landings which it was thought might be launched from Denmark or Norway. Certainly, any German troops landing in East Lothian would be able to drive quickly towards Edinburgh and, with the capital occupied, would be able to set up their military administration before advancing

7(b)

Anti-tank cubes at Aberlady

westwards to Glasgow and northwards toward the Highlands.

It was with this threat in mind that invasion defences were built in long lines across Aberlady Bay and Belhaven Bay. These obstacles would not stop an advancing tank, but would probably make it shed its tracks and certainly expose the thin armour on its vulnerable belly. Linked with these defences were minefields, with anti-personnel mines laid along the beaches from Aberlady to east of Dirleton. This formed part of the 'extended crust' of defences which stretched along probable invasion beaches, and were designed to stop minor attacks or delay larger invasions.

The second line of defences were road blocks which would be placed at junctions or narrow gorges where tanks would be unable to outflank the defences. These were to be manned by the Home Guard *(see 8a, 8b, 8c and 8d)* using Molotov cocktails and small arms, or whatever else was available.

As well as the strategic lines of defence, there were also defences built to protect what were classed as 'Vulnerable Points', such as aerodromes, radar stations, munitions factories, ammunition dumps, etc. Thus, R.A.F. Macmerry for example had a number of large pillboxes around the perimeter, of the standard type used on aerodromes and there was a small pillbox of a local design built on top of Berwick Law.

The threat of invasion from the air, rather than from the sea, was not forgotten and sawn-off tree trunks were embedded vertically in the beaches to prevent aircraft or gliders from landing on the long, flat stretches of sand.

7(c)

Anti-glider pole obstructions at Belhaven

Although the German invasion never came, the East Lothian defences were involved in invasion attempts, when training exercises were carried out in Gullane Bay in the spring of 1944. These exercises involved ships carrying supplies to Gullane from Leith, the supplies then being transferred to D.U.K.W.s (amphibious trucks) which would carry the supplies ashore. From a beach head established at Gullane, the supplies were loaded into army trucks which would return to Leith Docks, where their cargoes were loaded onto ships for the return journey. This training lasted for a period of about three weeks and proved of considerable value to the troops which landed in Normandy, since the beach they landed on at Asnelles was almost identical to Gullane Bay.

During these exercises some of the mines, anti-tank cubes and anti-glider poles were removed. During the period of this training much of East Lothian was included in an exclusion zone, entrance to which was not permitted to anyone who did not carry the correct pass.

In August 1963, with the Second World War long over, many of the anti-tank cubes were removed from Aberlady Bay. However, even now, fifty years after the end of the war, some can still be seen, to serve as a reminder of the time when East Lothian was threatened with invasion.

Eight

Home Guard

On 14 May 1940 the Secretary of State for War, Anthony Eden, broadcast an appeal on the B.B.C. Home Service for men aged between 17 and 65 to join the Local Defence Volunteers (L.D.V.) which was being formed. There was no shortage of men who wished to join the L.D.V. and a number of companies were established in East Lothian, including those at North Berwick *(see 8a)*, Aberlady *(see 8b)*, Broxburn *(see 8c)* and Macmerry *(see 8d)*. By the 15th, 100 men had volunteered at North Berwick and 15 in Gullane; by a week later the numbers had risen to 142 in North Berwick and 100 in Gullane. In fact the number of men who came forward meant that it was equipment and weapons which were in short supply, not volunteers, it being mid-June 1940 before uniforms became available. What weapons were available in the period following Dunkirk were in extremely short supply, but First World War rifles from the United States helped the motley collection of broom handles, pitch forks and antique hand-guns with which the L.D.V. were initially equipped.

Officially renamed the Home Guard on 23 July 1940, following a speech by Winston Churchill in which he referred to them by that name, much criticism has been directed at the L.D.V. regarding their usefulness. Probably due to the popular view of the Home Guard as bumbling fools which has resulted from the B.B.C. T.V. series Dad's Army, it has been claimed that had the German Army invaded Britain, the Home Guard would have been of little use and would have been decimated by the superior numbers and firepower of the invaders. However, closer study of the Home Guard reveals that it is unlikely that they would have been as ineffective as it might appear. In particular, the members of the Home Guard knew the local countryside - many were farmers, ploughmen or gamekeepers - and thus would have been able to use the terrain to their advantage, placing road-blocks and obstructions in the most favourable locations. As such, the Home Guard would have been able to delay the advance of German troops until such time as mobile reserves could hopefully counter-attack.

The use of such static defences *(see 7a and 7b)* would have been made more effective with

8(a)

North Berwick Home Guard Drilling on Esplanade

8(b)
Aberlady Home Guard

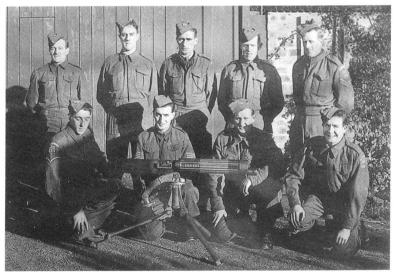

8(c)
Broxburn Home Guard

Guard started many members would have no ammunition at all, but by August 1943 it was estimated that Home Guard units in the Lothians and Peeblesshire held a total of almost half a million rounds of small arms ammunition, and this turned out to be an underestimate!

Prepared for an invasion that never came, much of the time spent by the members of the Home Guard was taken up with training. Such training required hard work and enthusiasm, both of which were in apparently plentiful supply. In September 1941 members of the 1st Battalion, East Lothian Home Guard, from Gullane, Dirleton and Aberlady held a weekend camp at the Hopes, near Gifford. Within a short space of time from their arrival in army trucks on the Saturday afternoon, tents had been erected, pits dug, a cook-house established, stores issued and they were ready for action. The afternoon and early evening were taken up by platoon exercises, patrolling, messages, communications, a talk on reconnaissance patrols by day and night, and in some ceremonial drill practice. The last activity was given particular emphasis when it was discovered that the camp was to be visited by a

the arrival from late 1940 of more and better weapons, such as Lewis machine-guns, Thompson sub-machine-guns, Mills Bombs (better known as hand grenades), Northover Projectors which could fire Molotov cocktails, and Spigot Mortars which were spring-fired anti-tank guns. Along with these weapons came increased stocks of ammunition. When the Home

8(d)
*Macmerry
Home Guard*

Field Marshall.

Mrs. Mary Stenhouse, a schoolchild living in the valley now occupied by the Whiteadder Reservoir, recalls:

The War Office decided we should have a branch of the Home Guard in the glen, so the Marquis of Tweeddale came as commander or whatever to organise the men. One young man had a motorbike so he was immediately elected dispatch-rider. The school-headmistress's husband was a retired gamekeeper so he was put in charge of the one gun: a double-barrel shotgun belonging to the Marquis. Various pieces of uniform were issued to whoever fitted them, though everyone got a tin-hat. A bonfire was built on Priestlaw Hill to be lit in case of invasion.

One older gentleman was stationed beside the one telephone in the glen. Early one Sunday morning his grandson came knocking at the window saying the invasion was expected any moment, whereby my father and the young shepherd who lodged with us went back to bed till their normal rising time. My father and the old gamekeeper with the one gun were to go on watch on Priestlaw Hill at 11.00 a.m., so after a quiet wander up the hill, they lay down in the shelter of a stone wall and lit their pipes to await the call to arms. An old cock grouse landed on the wall and perched there looking about, so the old man pointed the gun saying, "Man, John, what a grand shot that would be," at which my father told him not to fire or the whole of the south of Scotland would think the invasion had begun!

Stand down of the Home Guard finally came on Sunday 3 December 1944, with the need for a home defence clearly past. That day the East Lothian Battalion Home Guard held Stand Down parades. 'D' Company from Gullane were inspected by Colonel D. H. McCririck, Lothian and Borders Sub-Division Commander, and at 12.50 p.m. marched past the saluting base at the war memorial in the town, and into the history books as part of the preparations for the defence of Britain against an invasion which, thankfully, never took place.

Nine

Auxiliary Units (Resistance Units)

In the early summer of 1940, as German troops massed on the Channel coast of France in the aftermath of the Dunkirk evacuation, a secret organisation was formed, the members of which are only now, 50 years after the end of the Second World War, coming forward to admit its existence. It had been decided to form a British resistance network, which would carry out guerrilla warfare in the aftermath of a German invasion of Britain. Known as Auxiliary Units, these men would operate from carefully hidden operational bases, and although nominally members of the 201st Battalion, Home Guard, the existence of the Auxiliary Units was unknown to local Home Guard commanders. In fact, the 201st Battalion, which was the special Home Guard battalion for members of Auxiliary Units in Scotland, never appeared on the official Home Guard lists, and thus the men were never official members of a military unit and would not have been entitled to the protection afforded to all uniformed fighting men under the Geneva Convention. Knowing the ruthlessness of the Nazi regime, any members of Auxiliary Units who had fallen into enemy hands would undoubtedly have been executed.

What is not well known is that the Auxiliary Units were set up in Scotland, which was known as No. 1 Region, with headquarters undergound in East Lomond Hill in Fife. East Lothian was part of No. 4 (Border) Area, whose headquarters were given as "c/o G.P.O. Newtown St. Boswells, Roxburghshire and one of the best units in that area was the East Linton Patrol, which had its operational base at Janefield Wood *(see 9a)* with a communications base at Smeaton and a food store on Drylaw Hill. The hideouts were built by

9(a)
Janefield Wood operational base

All that was left of the World War II underground bunker at Janefield Wood near East Linton after an Army Bomb Disposal Unit had blown up around 200 lbs. of gelignite which was found in it.
'Courier' photo No. 2947.

troops brought north from England who were returned south immediately the work was completed.

The operational base (O.B.) at Janefield was built from corrugated iron sheets and measured roughly 20 feet by 12 feet, accessed by a vertical brick shaft. The O.B. contained six bunk beds, shelving and cupboard and it was to this underground hideout that members of the East Linton Patrol would have assembled when the invasion had taken place. Here their arms, ammunition and food would have been stored, ready for the time when East Lothian was under enemy occupation and the East Linton Patrol would emerge at night to carry out acts of sabotage, before disappearing back to the O.B., leaving no trace.

The communications base was to be the location from where messages would be sent and received, and this hideout was constructed of concrete with two rooms: one was for equipment and furniture, the other for communications equipment. Along one wall were pigeon holes containing booklets giving details of German units and equipment. In one pigeon hole was a concealed switch which could open a wall section to reveal a small annexe which contained the radio equipment *(see 9b)*. From there the operators, Mr. Alex Niven and Mr. James Grieve, were in contact with other radio operators in the Area.

In order to give the East Linton Patrol the skills they would have needed, extensive training was carried out. There were also Area competitions and a team from the East Linton Patrol, comprising Sergeant George Davidson and Privates Adam Middlemass and Charlie

9(b)
Mr Niven

Spence, came third place in the No. 4 (Border) Area Shooting Competition during July/August 1943. Sergeant Davidson achieved third place equal in the Individual Area Efficiency Tests by scoring 98.2%. Sergeant Davidson also gained first place in the Area in the Third Home Guard Patrol Competition, as a result of which he represented the Area in the semi-finals for Britain held at Coleshill House in Wiltshire, the headquarters of the Auxiliary Units organisation, subsequently coming third against units from all over the country.

In November 1944, with the invasion of North-West Europe going well, it was decided that there was no further need for the Auxiliary Units and, on 30 November 1944, word was sent out to all units to stand down. The British Resistance organisation, which was fortunately never put to the test, was disbanded.

Ten

Radio Security Service

The Radio Security Service (R.S.S.) was formed as part of the Security Service, also known as M.I.5. until being transferred to the Secret Service Intelligence, or M.I.6. in May 1941. The aim of the R.S.S. was to intercept radio signals produced by German spies and the German intelligence service, the Abwehr. A number of radio interception stations were built across Britain, with large aerial arrays and several huts.

In addition to such installations, the R.S.S. operated a large number of Voluntary Intercepts (V.I.s), part-time radio operators who would carry out the same function of monitoring radio frequencies for any unexpected transmissions, but operated using radio sets in their own homes. Any intercepted messages were forwarded to P.O. Box 25, Barnet, which was a cover address for the organisation. To provide additional cover, Volunteer Intercepts were issued with Royal Observer Corps uniform.

Despite such measures, the secrecy surrounding the R.S.S. was breached when an article on the work of the organisation appeared in the Daily Mirror on 14 February 1941. This article noted that "Britain's radio spies are at work every night...Home from work, a quick meal, and the hush-hush men unlock the door of a room usually at the top of the house. There, until the small hours, they sit, head-phones on ears, taking

10(a)

Mr Amos (below)

10(b)

Mr Coventry with H.M.S. Hood and Miss Couper

10(c)

Type of Receiver used

down the Morse code messages which fill the air."

Two East Lothian men were members of the Radio Security Service. Mr. Amos of Haddington and Mr. Coventry of North Berwick both carried out radio monitoring work. Mr William Amos carried out his work on equipment set up in the rear of his electrical shop in Market Street, Haddington, and both he and his shop assistant, Lizzie Tully-Jackson, had to sign the Official Secrets Act. Mr. Amos received the British Empire Medal in January 1946 in recognition of his services. However, the entry in The London Gazette notes that the award was to "William Alexander Amos, Observer, Royal Observer Corps," highlighting the fact that the real reason he received his award could not be outlined and mention could only be made of the cover organisation to which Voluntary Intercepts were ostensibly attached.

Eleven

Special Operations Executive

S.O.E., Belhaven School

11(a)

Staff on steps at Belhaven School

On 22 July 1940 the Special Operations Executive (S.O.E.) was formed by the War Cabinet as an independent secret service with the aim, as Churchill put it, to "set Europe ablaze." The new organisation was to be responsible for organising subversion and sabotage in enemy held territory overseas, working with the resistance groups in each country.

The work of S.O.E. relied on the ability of the organisation to maintain good communications links. Through such radio traffic S.O.E. was able to monitor events within Occupied Europe as

REMEMBER THE ENEMY IS LISTENING

11(b)

*Interior of
Belhaven School*

well as keeping in touch with its own agents in the field.

In order to carry out this vital work, in June 1943 Belhaven House in Dunbar was requisitioned, becoming Special Training School (S.T.S.) No. 54B.

Soon afterwards female radio operators, members of the First Aid Nursing Yeomanry (F.A.N.Y.) which was the cover body to which many of the female S.O.E. agents were ostensibly members, moved into Belhaven. From here the F.A.N.Y. radio operators kept in contact with agents and resistance groups in France and Norway. The Officer Commanding S.T.S. 54B at Belhaven, and thus responsible for this flow of radio traffic, was Major 'Pat' Patterson. The F.A.N.Y. officer was Ensign Margaret Daniels.

Belhaven House also played a vital role in training radio operators for S.O.E., being the second such school to open. As a result, trainees were able to send messages to Special Training School 54A at Fawley Court just north of Henley-on-Thames, over 300 miles away. Dealing with radio messages over such a distance gave the operators invaluable experience of receiving messages through interference. When agents in enemy territory sent messages, they were not in a position to repeat or clarify any distortions or words lost and it was therefore vital that both the sender and receiver were able to work to the highest possible degree of accuracy under what were usually very difficult conditions. The work of S.O.E. left no room for error, and it was at Belhaven House that the exacting training was given to the young women.

In July 1945, with the war in Europe over and victory soon to follow in the Far East, the Special Training School, now renumbered 52B, closed down.

Twelve

Tantallon

12(a)

Aerial View of A.S.E.E. Tantallon

In March 1944 scientists and technicians from Air Ministry and Admiralty research establishments arrived at Admiralty Signals Establishment Extension Tantallon. With the Allied invasion of France imminent, it was vital that techniques of jamming and deceiving German coastal radars were developed. Jamming the German radar stations would hide the approaching naval and airborne armada, and deception would make it appear that there was a vast fleet approaching France elsewhere.

Throughout March and April 1944 captured German Wurzburg and Seetaktradar sets, with British radars representing other German equipments, were involved in trials at Tantallon. Using a destroyer, mine-sweeper, Headquarters Ship, Fighter Direction Tender and several Landing craft and Motor Launches, various countermeasures equipments were tested against the German radars.

The Motor Launches were fitted with transmitters which meant they produced a signal on the radar screens equivalent to a destroyer. This meant it would be possible for a number of small boats to appear to the German radar operators to be a large fleet, thereby convincing them that the invasion was taking place away from the real landing beaches.

Another technique which was tested at Tantallon was the use of 'Window'. This consisted of bundles of aluminium strips which, when thrown out of an aircraft, reflected the radar signals and jammed the station. However, when carefully calculated amounts were dropped from an aircraft at specific intervals, 'Window' could make a single bomber appear to be a mass of aircraft, or even a fleet of ships. It was to check the theoretical calculations for these techniques that trials with 'Window' were carried out at Tantallon, using a B-25 Mitchell bomber to drop the reflective strips.

Immediately after the trials ended at Tantallon in late April, a further experiment was carried out on a radar station at Flamborough Head in Yorkshire which worked on the same wavelength as the Wurzburg radar to see if Radar Operators would report the deception as a convoy: they reported it as the biggest fleet they had seen. Thus proved, the techniques were planned for use on the night before the invasion by Stirling and Lancaster bombers of Nos. 218 and 617 Squadrons, the latter being the famous 'Dambusters'. The operations, given the codenames 'Glimmer' and 'Taxable' were a complete success as a result of extremely accurate flying and navigation, and contributed to the general confusion of the German

12(b)

German Wurzburg radar during trials at Tantallon in 1944

commanders in the immediate aftermath of the landings on 6 June 1944, which was of crucial importance to the success of D-Day. The deception and jamming operations tested at Tantallon, by strengthening the existing conviction of the German High Command that the invasion would take place in the Pas de Calais, rather than Normandy, also assisted with the deception operations to prevent the Germans sending reinforcements to Normandy.

As for the site at Tantallon, it continued to be used by the Admiralty for radar trials until being sold to Ferranti in 1984 although continuing in use for radar testing work until being closed down in 1994.

Thirteen

Fortitude North

The success of the Allied landings in Normandy on 6 June 1944, and the subsequent campaign to liberate Europe, was dependant on preventing reinforcements being brought into Normandy from the Russian Front as well as other occupied territories such as Greece, Yugoslavia and Norway.

As the nearest part of Britain to Norway, it was inevitable that Scotland would play a large part in ensuring that German troops, tanks, aircraft and shipping based in Norway remained there. In order to achieve this aim, it was decided that German intelligence should be led to believe that the Allies were planning to invade Norway from Scotland. This deception operation, named Fortitude North, was co-ordinated from Edinburgh Castle and consisted of a number of different schemes which, put together, would give the impression of the assembling of a large invasion force training for a Scandinavian campaign.

It was vital that it should appear to the Germans that a large force was being assembled, at a time when all available troops were being trained and organised for the real invasion to take place in Normandy. It was therefore necessary that a few troops should appear to be many, and this required extensive and elaborate deception schemes.

These plans involved units across the whole of Scotland, but the East Lothian area had a particularly central part in the deception schemes. What shipping was available was anchored in the Firth of Forth, including the harbours at Dunbar and North Berwick, the numbers of vessels in the area rising from 26 at the beginning of April 1944, to 71 by the middle of May. By 'allowing' German reconnaissance aircraft to photograph the ships and barges, since the ack-ack gunners had orders to put up a barrage but that the aiming should be very poor, Luftwaffe photo interpretation experts were led to believe that a large invasion fleet was being assembled.

However, since it could not be guaranteed that weather conditions would be suitable for reconnaissance aircraft at the intended times, more emphasis in Fortitude North was placed on bogus radio signals than visual deception. Since the real radio messages of an invasion force could not be sent, small units were used to send out the equivalent number of signals of a whole army. It was this deception which was based in East Lothian, the units involved operating out of Macmerry aerodrome *(see 1a, 1b and 1c)*.

The 52nd Mountain Division was involved in an exercise conducted without troops, using radios in vehicles under the control of officers who had orders to maintain normal tactical wireless traffic throughout the period of the exercise. Correct radio procedure was followed and standard coding practice carried out. It was only after the end of the war that the troops involved found out exactly what the purpose of the exercise had been.

In early 1944 Nos. 2737, 2830 and 2949 Squadrons, Royal Air Force Regiment *(see 13a*

13(a)
Deception Unit.
R.A.F. Regt., Macmerry

and 13b) were sent to Macmerry where they received training in mountain warfare and were issued with equipment for such work - boots, tents. One of the squadrons was even given snow shoes. Although the squadrons were eventually sent to Norway, leaving Leith on 14 May 1945, the mountain training they received was part of the deception operations.

Several books have criticised Fortitude North, claiming that it was ineffective and failed to convince the Germans to send reinforcements to Norway. However, the German garrison in Norway was maintained at 12 divisions, and thus no troops were sent from Norway to the fighting in Normandy. The arrival of such units in the early weeks of the landings might have crucially tipped the balance against the Allies, and thus Fortitude North, and the radio deception work carried out from Macmerry, was of considerable importance to the success of the Allies in the Second World War.

13(b) *Deception Unit. R.A.F. Regt., Macmerry*

Fourteen

War Production

Cunliffe-Owen Aircraft Works

14(a)
Cunliffe-Owen women workers at aircraft factory

14(b)
Cunliffe-Owen women workers at Gladsmuir Hall

Cunliffe-Owen Aircraft Limited had a factory just a few hundred yards outside the eastern perimeter of Macmerry aerodrome, which they used for modification and repair work on Lockheed Hudsons. This was the first aircraft built in the United States which was used by the R.A.F. in the Second World War and was operated by Coastal Command for maritime reconnaissance and anti-submarine patrol work.

The firm had been formed in 1937 as a subsidiary of the British American Tobacco Company at Eastleigh, near Southampton, to build the Burnelli Flying Wing aircraft under contract, and was renamed Cunliffe-Owen Aircraft Limited in May 1938.

The work at Macmerry was carried out by a large number of employees, most of whom were women, bussed in to the site by S.M.T. from all over East Lothian and the surrounding area.

Motor Launches

The yacht and boat building and design firm, William Weatherhead and Sons, had been building fishing boats from their yard in Cockenzie since 1880. In June 1940, along with a number of other firms, an order was placed with Weatherhead's for a construction of motor launches.

This work posed a number of problems for the firm, mainly due to the much larger size of a motor launch (M.L.) than a fishing boat; the keel of an M.L. was two and a half times longer than that of an average fishing boat. It was also discovered that the firm's shed at Cockenzie was too low and, rather than raise the roof, it was decided to excavate the floor, creating the extra space needed. The first ship completed was M.L.

168 and, being the first, it was decided that it should be given a traditional launch. However, further problems were created when orders were placed for more motor launches. The yard was too small in which to build more than one vessel at a time and therefore another shed was built on vacant land alongside, the firm carrying out the work itself as outside contractors could not give a completion date.

The increased workload for the yard meant that Weatherhead's had to take on many more workers, but with vastly increased shipbuilding during wartime, such skilled tradesmen were all in employment. As a result, the only solution was provided by the Ministry of Labour's local exchange which supplied joiners, although there

14(c)

Motor Launch under construction

14(d)

*Mr Weatherhead
with a naval officer*

was initially some confusion until the new tradesmen learned to convert "sharp end" and "blunt end" to "bow" and "stern" and all the other associated naval terms.

Weatherhead's was also given contracts for the construction of landing craft which required changes in building technique since they were made of steel plate. For a firm which had predominantly worked with wood, this was quite a change, but the challenge was successfully met, with one landing craft being built in 15 weeks.

The motor launches and landing craft were mainly prefabricated, the parts being supplied from Cobham in Surrey under the control of Fairmile Marine Company. The firm also built cabin cruisers for the War Office, these being used to transport army personnel to islands round Britain.

The great expansion of Weatherhead's during the war years saw the number of employees rise from 9 men to, at their peak, over 100 working on military contracts.

The workers were particularly pleased to receive a visit from some M.L. officers who had been in combat with German U-boats, the tales of their experience making the ship builders feel that they were really doing something for the war effort.

The Cockenzie fishing industry helped the war effort in other ways too. The local fishing fleet was commandeered by the Royal Navy and was used to patrol the Firth of Forth. These vessels became known as 'Harry Tate's Navy'.

Fifteen

They Also Served

Women's Land Army, Saltoun

15(a)
*Women's Land Army
Saltoun*

Within a few months of the outbreak of war in September 1939, 50,000 men had left the countryside, mostly Territorials called up or into better-paid factory work in the towns. As a result, there was a desperate need for agricultural labour to maintain domestic food production. Formed in June 1939, the Women's Land Army filled this need, providing between 80,000 and 90,000 farm workers at a time when female agricultural workers rose from being less than one tenth of the rural labour force to, by mid-1941, well over one quarter. The East Lothian

15(b)
*W.L.A. Saltoun
with soldiers*

Land Girls were housed in hostels at Eaglescairnie and other places right across the county.

Most of the land girls were from the countryside or rural towns, but nonetheless had a romantic notion of what the work involved, and were in for quite a shock. They were often surprised to find that it meant very early mornings, and hard, back-breaking, dirty work. What made the problems worse was that many, especially in the early part of the war, received little or no training, and were put to work on their first day. Rural conditions were generally primitive, with very little mechanisation, even after the flow of Lend-Lease agricultural equipment began. As late as 1943 the minority of farms had piped water and less than a quarter had electricity.

However, before long the girls and their hosts acclimatised to the culture clash and many ex-land girls look back on their wartime service as a time when they learned about the annual cycle beginning with seeding and ending in the harvest. Many enduring links were made in the small tight-knit rural communities. In the time off, the land girls enjoyed dances in village halls and helped in fund-raising events and many romances blossomed with local lads, resulting in many land girls settling in East Lothian to this day.

Another aspect of the wartime rural scene which is less well known is the collection of herbs, for which there was a great demand for medicinal purposes. Wartime restrictions limited the amount of herbs which could be imported and therefore native wild herbs became viable to collect. As a result members of the Whitekirk

W.R.I. set off in bicycling parties to gather what herbs grew locally. The village hall was used to dry the herbs, a wide variety of which were collected, from dock, coltsfoot and nettle, to elder, poppy petals and sunflowers. Once a quantity of herbs had been dried they were packed separately in sacks and then weighed and labelled, before being sent by rail to a London firm, which paid anything up to perhaps £12 per consignment, the money always being donated by Whitekirk W.R.I. to the Red Cross.

East Lothian also saw other agricultural activity in the form of the collection of sphagnum moss from the Lammermuir Hills which, once cleaned and dried, could be used in medical dressings. Also gathered were rosehips, the syrup from which was a very good source of vitamin C for children.

Haddington Canteen

15(c)

Haddington Canteen Workers

A canteen set up by the combined churches in the Holy Trinity Hall in Haddington, providing a place where the troops based in the vicinity could go for a much welcomed cup of tea, something to eat, as well as a chat. The canteen provided a place where servicemen could relax and socialise, and perhaps pick up a date for the evening. There was also a canteen in the High Street, organised by the W.R.I.

British Honduras Forestry Workers

15(d)

British Honduras Forestry Workers

During the Second World War there was a huge demand for timber. It was required for pit props, required in vast numbers for the coal industry which fuelled steel production and hence armaments; hutting for the services; radio towers; as well as to repair bomb damage to buildings and railways. This increased demand came at a time when overseas supplies of timber (mainly from Canada) were severely curtailed. It was therefore necessary to increase domestic production and to do so required labour at a time when there was a severe labour shortage.

The solution came from British Honduras (now Belize) and, when volunteer workers were asked for in 1941, 900 came forward to help, despite tales of how cold it would be compared to

their home. Some of them had even been told that it was so cold in Britain that the words would freeze as they came out of one's mouth, and they would have to be melted in a frying pan before anyone could hear what had been said! Most had not seen snow before, although it was not long after their arrival in October 1941 that they were able to enjoy the new experience. It did take the men from British Honduras some time to acclimatise, one man even resorting to sleeping with 14 blankets that winter!

The forestry workers were used to the giant hardwood trees at home and compared to these, the smaller softwood trees in East Lothian seemed like "matchsticks." Nonetheless, the work they carried out was of vital importance to the war effort and more and more men were gradually brought over from British Honduras, another 400 arriving in November 1942.

Their life in Scotland was not all work, however, and one group formed a band which played at Tranent, whose musical skills were much appreciated. They were also considered very good dancers, a skill to which local girls took very kindly. This partly explains why the second contingent of forestry workers were sent to remote areas of the Highlands! Some of the men were repatriated in December 1943, but others stayed on in Scotland, some of them marrying local girls.

A.F.S., Haddington

15(e)
*A.F.S.
Haddington*

In the summer of 1940 the Auxiliary Fire Service (A.F.S.) was formed to augment the regular fire service, there being units in Haddington (see 15e), Gullane (with a two-man manual pump housed in Dirleton) and elsewhere in the county. The A.F.S. provided a vital service in East Lothian, dealing rapidly with any fires and also giving lectures to local groups on subjects such as how to deal with incendiary bombs.

Evacuees

15(f)

Evacuees

With the threat of devastation from the air which had become part of military planning in the 1930s, it was decided that, in the event of war, it would be necessary to evacuate children from all cities and industrial centres. Detailed planning for the evacuation of children from Edinburgh began in early 1939, although of 33,150 households which took part in a survey to assess the level of interest in evacuation, only 12,642 families noted that they wished to participate.

When Germany invaded Poland on 1 September 1939, the official evacuation scheme was launched, with 26,000 leaving Edinburgh, just over 40% of those entitled to be evacuated. The reception areas for Edinburgh children ranged from Inverness to the Borders, with two evacuation camps set up at Broomlee, near West Linton, and Middleton, near Gorebridge. Children were also sent to East Lothian which was considered a safe distance from the capital, even though the early actions of the war were to take place in the skies over East Lothian.

However, it was not the possible dangers from such attacks which saw children return to the city, but the clash of cultures as city children encountered an entirely different way of life in the country. They considered rural life to be backward and primitive without any modern comforts; whilst their hosts often considered the children to be dirty and ill-behaved layabouts. By March 1940, even though 100 children were being sent from Edinburgh every week, only 9,968 children remained outside the city. Clearly the pull of home was much stronger than any official orders!

Sixteen

Fund Raising

H.M.S. Dunbar and Comforts Fund

In order to help finance the war effort, and also make the people on the 'Home Front' feel they were involved in the war, civilians were encouraged to raise as much money as possible to pay for munitions and supplies which had to be paid for in hard currency.

In November 1941 the War Savings Committee decided that more money would be raised through voluntary efforts if the people raising money could identify exactly where their money was being spent. As a result, it was decided to offer communities the chance to sponsor an aircraft or ship, etc., which would then be named by the community which had paid for it. The schemes were launched in weeks in which targets were set which would cover the cost of producing a particular weapon. In 1943 there was "Wings for Victory Week," East Lothian being given a target of £400,000 and actually raising £532,130! "War Weapons Week" in 1941 had raised a total of £252,000, more than two and a half times the target of £100,000.

From 28 February to 7 March 1942 was

16(a)

H.M.S. Dunbar

16(b)

*Back green
concert party for
Comforts Fund*

"Warship Week" and East Lothian was given a target sum of £250,000. So successful was this fund-raising effort that a total sum of £357,148 6s 1d was donated.

As a result of the success of "Warship Week" in East Lothian, the county was able to adopt a Bangor Class mine-sweeper, which had been built by Blyth Shipbuilding & Dry Dock Company and launched on 5 June 1941, the vessel being named H.M.S. Dunbar.

Following a request from the ship, the Dunbar Town Council presented the mine-sweeper with a plaque of the town's coat of arms, which was fitted to the bridge of the ship and was carried by

her on her wartime duties. These duties included mine-sweeping operations around Iceland and the west coast of Scotland and escort duties in the Mediterranean during 1942 and mine-sweeping during the Normandy landings in June 1944.

East Lothian residents also raised large sums of money for other causes, including the Comforts Fund which was formed to send warm, woollen clothing, cigarettes, food, etc. to servicemen overseas. Not only would such gifts help ease the living conditions of frontline personnel, but would also let them know that the people at home were thinking of them, knowledge vital to maintaining their morale.

Seventeen

Royal Train

The outbreak of the Second World War brought hectic schedules to the daily life of the Royal Family. King George VI and Queen Elizabeth toured the length and breadth of the country, visiting people at their homes and workplaces giving them a much-needed morale boost. For the lengthy trips such touring involved, heavy use was made of the Royal Train and from 1941 onwards this included two new saloon cars - Nos. 798 and 799 - for the King and Queen respectively.

However, the war brought a new threat to the security of the Royal couple, that of air attack on the Royal Train. As a result, when the train was 'stabled' overnight near to the location of the next day's tour, it was taken near to a railway tunnel for added protection, the engine steamed-up ready to seek the refuge of the tunnel in the event of an air-raid warning being issued.

It was such precautionary measures which led to the Royal Train frequently being brought up the branch line to Aberlady in the middle of the night, where the Royal Family could sleep restfully in more secure surroundings than central Edinburgh. From the security of Aberlady, the train would then head for Waverley Station in Edinburgh where the King and Queen would carry out their official duties, being met at the station by the Lord Provost.

As would be expected in view of such frequent Royal visits, Aberlady Station was repainted and the station surroundings kept clean and tidy. Large numbers of C.I.D. officers from Edinburgh would be present at Aberlady whilst the Royal Train was there, ensuring the complete safety of the Royal passengers, although the influx of so many policemen meant that the Royal Train was something of an open secret in the village. The use of Aberlady Station by the Royal Train is understood to have continued for several years after the end of the war.

The King and Queen were also in the area when they visited Drem, as they did on 28 February 1940, when the Air Officer Commander-in-Chief of Fighter Command, Sir Hugh Dowding, and the A.O.C. of No. 13 Group, Air-Vice Marshal Saul, were presented to the King. The Commanding Officer of No. 602 Squadron, Wing Commander Douglas Farquhar was presented with the Distinguished Flying Cross by the King on that occasion.

17(a)

King George VI at Drem presenting medals

17(b)
Aberlady Station

17(c)
Royal Train

Eighteen

Polish Army

The invasion of Poland by German forces on 1 September 1939, the action which began the war in Europe, was to have direct consequence for East Lothian. After the collapse of Poland under the weight of a combined attack from Germany and, from 17 September, the Soviet Union, what units of the Polish armed forces were able to escape, sought exile in France. The fall of France in June 1940 proved a bitter blow to the Poles, who lost their closest ally. However, having pledged to fight on, the Poles left France; by 18 July 1940 almost 17,000 had arrived in Britain.

During the initial few months in Scotland, the Polish troops shared the problems of lack of weapons and equipment faced by all units in Britain. However, eventually they organised and equipped themselves, forming new units in anticipation of the time when they would return to continental Europe and liberate their homeland.

Having experienced first-hand the German blitzkrieg tactics of rapid armoured attacks, the Polish Army appreciated the great importance of armoured units and the use of tanks in modern warfare. It was also realised that if Poles were to play a significant part in the invasion of Europe, the army in Scotland would have to include an armoured formation. In consequence, in February 1942 the 1st Polish Armoured Division was established, with General Stanislaw Maczek as its Commanding Officer. Many of the units which were part of the division were based in East Lothian. In March 1942 the 10th Mounted Rifles (an armoured regiment), part of the 10th Armoured Cavalry Brigade, arrived in Haddington where it would stay for about 14 months. Until the summer of 1942 the regiment was equipped with only a few old Polish light tanks and it was only later that a few Valentine tanks were issued.

During their time at Haddington the 10th Mounted Rifles were given thorough training, the instructors being sent on courses to English training centres, and also received more modern tanks in the form of Covenanters and then Crusader Mk. III Cruiser tanks (*see 18a and 18b*). Much of the training took place up on the

18(a)
Polish tanks leaving Amisfield Park

18(b)
Polish tanks at station

18(c)
Group of Poles at Gifford Post office

Lammermuir Hills, which provided the vast space needed for tank manoeuvres and training in the techniques of mobile armoured warfare which it was hoped would be put to good use after the invasion of Europe.

Mrs. Mary Stenhouse, a schoolchild living in the valley now occupied by the Whiteadder Reservoir, recalls Polish tanks training in the vicinity:

Polish soldiers tried to make tanks climb walls or dry-stane dikes. The devastation was unreal. As they came towards us the noise of the tank tracks on tarred roads could be heard miles away like thunder. They practised shelling on Mayshiel and Faseny and our father had sometimes to meet us from Kingside School as it was very frightening for two little girls.

18(d)
*Poles at Lady Kitty's
Garden, Haddington*

In February 1943 the 10th Mounted Rifles were presented with a flag and also a scroll bearing the signatures of the members of the Haddington branch of the Scottish-Polish Society. These presentations were made to commemorate the stay of the unit in Haddington. In May 1943 the 10th Mounted Rifles finally left Haddington for training grounds near Newmarket.

The story of the Polish forces in East Lothian is not, however, limited to ground units. No. 307 Squadron operated from Drem between November 1943 and March 1944 with Mosquito night fighter aircraft and No. 309 Squadron also flew from Drem *(see 1e)*, with Hurricane and Mustang fighters for day defence from April to November 1944. There were also great numbers of Polish aircrew under training at East Fortune *(see 1d)*, an experience which cost many of them their lives.

Mr. Edward Sanetra was one of the Polish airmen who flew from East Fortune, as a test pilot for No. 289 Squadron, an anti-aircraft co-operation unit. Mr. Sanetra, a Sergeant in the R.A.F., received the Air Force Cross and was mentioned in dispatches as well as receiving special honour from Poland, in recognition of his wartime service.

However, the story of the Polish forces in East Lothian is not simply a catalogue of the units based in the county. The links which were forged at that time between the Poles and the local inhabitants are a more enduring indication of the Polish wartime presence. The Poles, with their exemplary manners and unusual accents, proved irresistible to many local girls and the marriages

18(e)
*Polish General
in Gifford*

which took place resulted in many Polish servicemen settling in East Lothian, and the extensive Polish community, now fully integrated into Scottish society, is a continuing reminder of those dark days. More formal links were created with the establishment in April 1941 of the Scottish-Polish Society, designed to promote better relations between the Polish servicemen and the Scottish communities in which they were based. The activities organised by the various branches were quite 'high-brow' in nature, with educational and cultural activities. The society proved popular.

Nineteen

Gosford Camp

In 1940 Gosford House was taken over by the War Office for use as a billet for troops. The King's Own Scottish Borderers spent a considerable period of time at Gosford, and many huts were erected to house the large numbers of men based there. The K.O.S.B. were part of 155th Brigade, 52nd Division, which also included the 7th/9th Royal Scots, the latter also spending many months in the Gullane area.

The large number of German prisoners being taken following the Normandy landings in June 1944 meant that an expansion of P.o.W. facilities was required. Consequently, in 1944 Gosford Camp became Camp No. 16, a prisoner of war camp for around 3,000 German troops. The prisoners were accommodated 50 men to each hut but even then the vast numbers held there meant that until Christmas 1944, when numbers

19(a)

Gosford Camp
Canteen

19(b)
Gosford Camp
raw recruits

19(c)
Gosford Camp
German P.O.W.s 1944

in the camp were reduced, approximately 400 men had to sleep on palliasses in tents. Despite this, provision was made to make life as comfortable as possible for the prisoners. The facilities at the camp included a theatre, a cinema, a football pitch and a sports ground. There was also a camp band with 30 musicians playing a wide variety of instruments. A number of the prisoners with artistic talents painted various scenes in the hut and many views of home towns were drawn from memory. Small gardens were made in front of the huts which also helped improve the living conditions.

Every day, at 6.00 a.m. and 6.00 p.m., a roll-call was taken with all 3,000 men standing in 6 rows on the main camp road. The roll-call was taken by a British officer and four soldiers and was probably considered a routine procedure

Twenty

Amisfield P.o.W. Camp

In 1944 the Prisoner of War camp was set up at Gosford Camp, and was to hold around 3,000 men, in conditions which were somewhat overcrowded. As a result, a satellite camp, No. 16A, was opened at Amisfield, near Haddington. A much smaller compound, this camp held the extra men for which there was insufficient capacity at Gosford.

Mr. Harry Dittrich, who arrived at Gosford Camp in 1944 was sent to Camp 16A at Amisfield after a few weeks, along with all the other non-Germans, a total of 800 men. He recalls:

"I spent two years there. We had to work on farms but it was a nice camp, very tidy and run by ourselves. We had a theatre and a good band,

20(a)

Camp at Amisfield

plays were written and concerts laid on frequently. Many of the Austrians came from Vienna: music and song were in their blood and what they had to offer was really outstanding. I had lots of friends among them.

During those two years I had the first opportunities of closer contact with the local population and getting a picture of life in Scotland. I was very impressed by what I saw. It was such a peaceful and friendly land, entirely different from what I had known on the continent. Of course, I had difficulties with the language at first, but I soon started to pick up a few words here and there.

After two years in Haddington the camp was closed. We were sent back to the main camp in Gosford and that's where the trouble started. After two years of comparative freedom, with hardly a wire round our camp, we were suddenly confronted by our old friends the German army sergeants, ordering us about. We couldn't believe our eyes. It looked as if nobody had told them that the war was long finished. They strutted about in their uniforms, covered in medals. I had never seen so many Iron Crosses in my life. We found out later that they had all been fashioned out of tin from the cook-house and handpainted. The only thing missing in that camp was the old Hitler salute; it was unbelievable! And the majority of them were still Nazis. The old sergeants went hysterical when we told them we weren't in the German army anymore. We refused to follow their orders, all one thousand of us. The guard had to be called out, bugles were blown and I believe even the fire brigade were there, but they couldn't do a thing with us. Most of us 'foreigners' and trouble-makers were transferred to other camps up and down the country as soon as possible after that."

After the end of hostilities many Ukrainian ex-P.o.W.s spent some time at Amisfield Camp prior to release into the community.

20(b)
Prisoners of War at Amisfield Camp

Twenty-one

Welcome Home

The unconditional surrender of Germany, signed on 7 May 1945 and celebrated the following day, V-E Day, was greeted with joy and relief throughout Britain, although there was still the realisation that the war in the Far East was yet to be won. Only the surrender of Japan on 14 August, with V-J Day the day after, finally saw the Second World War over.

For some, the victory was a time of rejoicing, a celebration of the triumph of democracy over tyranny or just the lifting of some of the wartime restrictions. For others, it was a sombre occasion, a time to remember loved ones who would never return. For most, though, it meant that it would not be much longer before their husband, boyfriend, son or father returned home.

Thousands of East Lothian men served in the forces at home and overseas and, with the

21(a)
*Chrissy Bathgate
with accordion*

outbreak of peace, anxiously waited to exchange their uniforms for 'civvies' and the infamous Demob suit and to return home. These men, who had served their country with distinction and faced horrors which cannot possibly be imaginable by those who were not there, were treated as heroes and returned to be guests of honour at civic ceremonies and 'Welcome Home' parties, often receiving the freedom of their home towns.

The war that these men sacrificed so much to help win has proved to be the 'war to end wars' that the First World War was not. In the 50 years since the end of the Second World War we have been lucky enough not to face another world war and have been spared the horrors that the servicemen and women, and their families, went through from 1939 until 1945.

21(b)

Welcome home party, Haddington Town Hall

21(c)

Demob Suits - men lined up wearing them

Bibliography

Brown, Ian, et al, *20th century Defences in Britain* Council for British Archaeology 1995.

Bunyan, I. T., et al, *East Fortune: Museum of Flight and History of the Airfield* Royal Scottish Museum 1983.

Carswell, Allan *For Your Freedom and Ours* National Museums of Scotland 1993.

Cox, Michael (ed.), *Two Villages at War* Gullane and Dirleton Historical Society 1995.

Foot, M. R. D., *S.O.E.* British Broadcasting Corporation 1984.

Howard, Michael *British Intelligence in the Second World War Volume 5* H.M.S.O. 1990.

Jeffrey, Andrew *This Present Emergency* Mainstream Publishing Company (Edinburgh) Ltd 1992.

Johnstone, Sandy, Air Vice-Marshal *Spitfire into War* William Kimber & Co. Ltd. 1986.

Lampe, David *The Last Ditch* Cassell 1968.

Longmate, Norman *The Real Dad's Army* Arrow Books Ltd. 1974.

Ramsey, Winston G. (ed.), *After the Battle 76* Battle of Britain Prints International Ltd. 1992.

Smith, David J. *Action Stations 7* Patrick Stephens Ltd. 1983.

Smith, David J. *Britain's Military Airfields 1939-1945* Patrick Stephens Ltd. 1989.

Strachura, Peter D. (ed.), *Themes of Modern Polish History* The Polish Social and Educational Society 1992.

Thetford, Owen *Aircraft of the Royal Air Force since 1918* Putnam & Co. Ltd. 1979.

West, Nigel *Secret War* Hodder & Stoughton 1992.

Wood, Derek *Attack Warning Red* Carmichael and Sweet Limited 1992.